MW00443233

The Six Biggest Tax Mistakes That Physicians Make

By Ken Himmler

Copyright © 2016 by Ken Himmler, AAB Agency, LLC and Blue Apple Entertainment, LLC. All rights reserved worldwide. No part of this publication may be replicated, redistributed, or given away, in any form without the prior written consent of the author or publisher.

Blue Apple Entertainment, LLC
11700 W Charleston Blvd Ste. 170-519
Las Vegas, NV 89135

No part of this book should be considered investment, tax, estate planning or risk protection advice. This book is for educational purposes only. Please contact either a fiduciary advisor, a lawyer, CPA or insurance agent if you consider putting any part of this book into action.

ISBN-10:0-9976101-0-7
ISBN-15:978-0-9973101-0-9

Library of Congress Number: 2016907990

U.S. Copyright Registration: May 2016

Table of Contents

Introduction

My name is Ken Himmler and for the last thirty-plus years I've been working with physicians and Medical Groups. This work focuses on improving the physicians' financial future by reducing taxes and restructuring their businesses and investments.

I've been asked over and over again by my physician clients to write a book just for physicians. With raising a family and working with my current clients I couldn't seem to find the time.

I recently had an experience that changed all that. I met with a physician who'd been practicing for forty years and wanted to retire but felt he couldn't.

This physician was seventy-two years old so I asked him why he was still working. He responded by telling me he had no way of knowing how he could afford to retire.

After looking through his taxes, investments and trusts, I could see why he thought this.

His plan was a total mess. He was overpaying on his income taxes by over $100,000 a year. His investments, all with a broker, had average fees of 3.2% and he hadn't updated his Trusts in years.

1

With this kind of team working for him, who needs enemies?

At that meeting, I decided I would find the time to put together a short book on some of the biggest mistakes I've seen physicians make.

This book is motivated out of my utter frustration and despair I've seen with poor advice given to physicians. I couldn't take it anymore. I had to do something about what I was seeing.

Before we get started, it makes sense to explain why I might be able to help you.

First, I understand the landscape of what's going on in the physician's world of money.

Second, I've been working with physicians for thirty-plus years. I understand the hectic, stressful and chaotic lifestyles of the medical profession.

My beginnings were in Buffalo, New York. I was working with first and second year residents and attending physicians coming through the University of Buffalo Medical School. I also dealt with some of the more mature physicians from Erie County Medical Center along with many of the integrated doctors that were not only practicing but also teaching at the University of Buffalo.

Back then, a large part of my practice was comprised of professional athletes, celebrities and physicians. At that time, physicians were the highest earning professionals in the United States.

Starting around the mid-1980s I noticed a deep jealousy and disdain developing towards the income the medical profession was earning.

I also noticed changes with Congress which were implemented and enforced by insurance companies that would further reduce the career benefits of physicians.

As time went on, Medicaid and Medicare went deeper and deeper into the financial abyss. The Government found it necessary to recover their losses on the backs of the medical professionals by reducing reimbursements and pushing the paperwork and compliance load to the doctor's office.

I watched as physician's lifestyles declined while the number of hour's physicians worked increased. There was an increase in liability and lawsuits. The amount of paperwork requirements and regulations dramatically increased.

The result was a decrease in the pay per hour and less motivation for younger people to go after this beloved career.

Now it seems every year, physicians are working harder and harder to make the same amount of income, protect themselves from lawsuits and still have a family life.

We, as their Planners have to work even harder at trying to protect physicians and their money from taxes, lawsuits and even employment theft from their staff.

After writing a multitude of other books, I thought it was time to describe what I've seen from an insider/outsiders point of view on a physician's financial security.

This book is dedicated to every one of you that made the decision to serve your fellow man, take the oath and commit thousands of hours to learning and training and subjecting yourself to all the liability, lawsuits, long hours and reduced pay.

I hope this book gives you some direction on how to hold onto more of what you earn, protect it, grow it and use it to enjoy your life.

How to Use This Book

When I decided to write this book, I wanted to put together something that wasn't only informative and educational but also interactive.

The challenge with today's books is we're all so busy. We read a book and learn great new ideas, then life gets in the way. We forget these ideas and we go back to living. We know there's things we can do to improve our lives but we don't do them because we don't have the time.

I should write a book called Time, The New Currency. For a physician, time seems to be their most valuable asset.

As my first boss instructed me, time is the only asset you can spend but never earn again.

If you're anything like me, you might read a book and learn some great new ideas. Then, when you're ready to implement them, you don't know who to turn to or the first step to take.

Please don't worry, I'll not leave you hanging and wondering how or if you can implement some of these ideas.

The first step is to read this book to understand what some of the ideas are that might save you tax.

The second step is, if you learn you're missing out on some of these strategies, you can get a complimentary thirty-minute phone consultation with one of our tax-planning specialists.

If we find you might have an opportunity to save tax, the consultant will give you the instructions on how to get us the hard data so we can make an absolute analysis.

If we find you can't use any of these ideas but we see other strategies with investment, insurance, practice management, asset protection or retirement planning, our consultants will refer you to someone that may be able to help you.

Twenty years ago, I would've told you we would refer you to someone near you.

Today, we have the technology to bring talent closer. We can now scan our tax returns and have a top tax planner look at it from across the country, make an analysis and even structure a recommendation.

No longer are we handcuffed to the talent that only lives near us. Now, we can get the most talented practitioners in just about any field no matter where they live.

I tell you this because we have clients around the world and we work seamlessly with them on complex money matters.

Don't limit yourself to talent just because you think you have to personally go and visit them.

From my experience, physicians are the busiest people in the world. Why take time to go meet someone during office hours when you can have a web-based meeting, communicate through email or even have a web-based financial planning program completed for you?

Even in traditional academia there's technology with online videos, online quizzes and almost an infinite availability of resources.

Due to the licenses and certifications I hold I must personally complete over 120 hours a year in continuing education. I've not gone to a physical classroom to get these hours in over ten years.

I go to conferences each year but mainly to socialize with colleges and listen to world class speakers.

The base knowledge of almost any discipline can now be delivered in very efficient and controllable methods without having to go to a location.

With these resources available, I wanted to make this book a beginning point and a reference you can use to expand your knowledge base along with your financial net worth.

There are nine chapters in this book. I've intentionally kept these chapters short and to the point to help you understand what the problems are and what some of your potential solutions might be.

Taxes, investments and financial planning change on a daily basis. To keep up with those changes I've created an information and education site you can access to keep up to date on new strategies. That site is kenhimmler.com/trf

There's also a blog in which you can join. I write weekly posts based on recent developments in the personal finance area. You can access that site by going to kenhimmler.com/blog

You can also go to this same site and there's a pay-per-view classroom. You can take an online course taught by yours truly on everything from income tax reduction, asset protection and even investment strategies.

These courses cost anywhere between $49.00 and $3,000 but can get into much more detail and granularity than I could ever hope to do in a blog post.

This book is only a starting point because it will help you identify some of the potential opportunities, but it can't give you detailed advice on how you should structure your personal tax plan.

Before taking action on any of the ideas I discuss I need to give you a warning.

To explain my warning, I'll take you back to my old radio show days. After a period on the radio, you get a lot of people taking ideas given on air but they don't follow through with the ideas properly.

Even though I'd give the warnings to only work with a qualified financial planner, some still took the leap to do it on their own or dealt with salespeople or brokers.

I would occasionally get people calling back in and say they'd listened to something I discussed on air and it didn't work for them.

I'd ask them what steps they took to accomplish this strategy? In every case, where it didn't work out it was because they either left a step out, didn't follow the steps properly or completely changed the order of the steps.

This doesn't differ from you performing a surgical procedure and deciding at the last minute you're going to change the order and procedure of your operation. I'm sure you would agree you'd have devastating results. I'll bet your surgical team wouldn't be happy with you either.

Therefore, this is my disclaimer. While I have good intentions to help you understand what some of the mistakes are that physicians make with their taxes, this is not intended to be tax advice, legal advice or financial advice of any manner.

In real estate they teach the three keys to success are location, location, location.

In a successful financial, retirement or tax planning we have our three rules too. Those three rules are CALCULATE, CALCULATE, CALCULATE!

I also may offer suggestions as to what the solutions to these identifiable tax problems are. This is not meant to tell you this is what you need to do.

To get the full effect of legal tax deductions you need to follow the IRS's rules. In addition, make sure you do the calculations to assure that whatever you spend to get advice or take any action has a profitable outcome for you.

The last item I want to cover is making sure your mind is open to looking at new ideas.

Finances and talking about finances can be as sensitive as talking about religion or politics. Finances and the success or failure thereof can bring out the best and the worst in people.

While I don't hold a medical degree and have no medical basis in saying this other than experience, my opinion is having a sound and secure financial future can improve your health.

To help understand why I say this let me share with you my opinion on what I've experienced over thirty years of practice.

I've seen extremely successful physicians and also complete financial failures.

Your financial success is dependent more on how you think and make financial decisions than it is on how smart you are.

Your financial success will depend a small part on your medical discipline and where you live, but not as much as how you think about money.

My best example is when I'm public speaking. I ask the crowd to fill the in blank – Money doesn't grow on _____.

Did you say trees? If you said trees, where did you get that from? Did you get it from your parents? If you did, you've been conditioned to think about money from your parents?

Some statistics say that over 80% of our religious, political and financial beliefs are passed down from our parents.

Think about your parent's financial success. Do you want to be like your parents?

If your parents were financially successful, you may already have a good foundation for making sound financial decisions.

If your parents struggled with money, your money beliefs might be built on a faulty foundation.

When I was on the radio, I would test people on air and ask them about their financial beliefs.

When we discovered a lost opportunity, a bad investment decision or a financial disaster we would try to identify why.

It was interesting to find in every case the reason for these disasters always led back to some belief system or conditioning of the person.

Let's stop for a minute. You might be thinking, "wait a minute, I thought this was a book on how to reduce my income tax."

It is such a book.

However, with this book I want you to profit by 100% to 1000% of what you've spent.

I know the only way I can improve someone's financial future is to get someone to accept a new, different or alternative way to think.

I also know people can be prevented to a new way of thinking when they're holding onto old belief systems or conditioning.

Let me give you an example of some of the things I've heard that have prevented people from making, saving or protecting thousands if not millions of dollars for themselves.

1. My accountant says it's not the way he does it.
2. My stockbroker says it's outside the scope of what they can do in tax structure.
3. If this works then why have I not heard about it before? This is my favorite. This would be like a doctor telling his patient about a new drug or procedure and the patient says "why haven't I heard of that before?"
4. It's not worth the time
5. I don't want to raise any red flags with the IRS
6. I'll get to it next year
7. My accountant said he's too busy during tax season
8. I don't want to put a burden on my bookkeeper

I suppose I could go on and on with all the things I've heard over the years. The bottom line is when your mind is open to improvement, change, and alternatives then and only then can you improve.

If you're not open to change, it will never happen.

One of the other reasons I've found physicians don't get the most out of their money is the term I've coined as "financial arrogance."

Financial arrogance is when someone thinks they know it all. It could be the person who's the internet researcher that knows better than the practitioner.

Maybe one of the worst and best things which has happened in the medical field is the internet. Sites like WebMD can help physicians with medical research quickly. These same sites also give the patient a little bit of knowledge, which is sometimes very dangerous.

Have you ever had a patient come to you and say "I've read this or that on the internet"? How about this one, "I think I have this disease because I have all the symptoms listed on the internet"? If you've had this experience, you've probably had the thought, "oh boy here we go, now I have to help them unlearn what they think they know".

There's a lot of similarities between a financial counselor and a physician when it comes to trying to help people for a living.

Whether you work with one of our consultants or you find your own, please allow me to give you one piece of advice which will serve your well.

Always keep an open mind. Don't immediately discount an idea. Instead, adopt a CEO's thinking on any idea and ask the following questions.

1) If I employ this idea, how much after expenses will this save or make for me in a year?
2) If I employ this idea, what are my risks in time and cost?
3) If I employ this idea, and it doesn't work, how much will it cost me?
4) If I employ this idea and it works, how much in total over the next five or ten years can I expect to save or make?
5) How much total administrative time will this take me? (Remember, time is the new currency)

Please don't discount any idea until you've quantified and qualified it.

If you come to the table with an old belief or an incorrect belief, then you immediately count yourself out of that idea.

The last part I want to cover is what you can do to make sure you're not paying more tax than you should.

You must be working with a top end tax planner and not just a tax preparer.

You'll know the difference because a top end tax planner is working on ideas every quarter of the year.

These should be new ideas and should be mathematically tested.

If your tax person isn't coming to you at least two to four times throughout the year, I would submit you have a tax preparer and not a tax planner.
These two jobs are very different.

Now let's get into the meat of what this book is going to teach you.

CHAPTER 1.... WHY REDUCE TAXES?

The question of the century is why take any time to reduce taxes.

In my opinion, we live in what I would consider the best country in the world. Unfortunately, our tax system is still wrought with inequities and unfairness.

Our tax system looks more like the Spanish Inquisition than a tax code.

Taxes started during the Civil War when it was required to raise funds under Abraham Lincoln's leadership. Since then the tax code has expanded to what is now the world's largest single written document.

The tax code creates more than **450 changes** every year.

The last three decades in practice I've seen certain tax issues waffle back and forth from year-to-year. This makes it almost impossible for anyone that's not in this profession, and even for some of those in the profession, to follow all the rules, understand them and to be able to take advantage of them.

To add insult to injury, the tax code is anything but fair. There are so many rules which cost us the citizen penalties and interest. When the government violates the same rules, there's no penalty.

I believe it's a one-sided game which could, under different circumstances, be changed to be fair and equitable for everyone.

If you own a business, the rules are even more complex. In recent years the government has increased taxes and complexity to the point companies want to leave the United States.

Corporate tax rules and rates cost hundreds of thousands of jobs to overseas countries who understand how to attract and keep corporations and jobs. The corporate tax problem is an entirely different matter that could use a book of their own.

You may be self-employed so we'll also go into some of the mistakes physicians make in their practices. These ideas may help you not only reduce personal income taxes but taxes related to your business.

The big question is; why should I reduce my income tax? While this might sound like a rhetorical question, I'll bring it back to the logic in the mathematics. Over your life, the largest expense will be your taxes.

As an example, your FICA taxes are a triple taxed item. This means **you will pay 15.3%** if you're self-employed for your FICA and you'll get taxed two more times on the same money.

<u>In the United States, more than 33% of taxpayers pay more in Social Security and Medicare than they do in Federal Income Taxes.</u>

Add these high taxes onto Obamacare and you have an even higher tax environment. Now there's even more taxes to fund the new costs associated with ACA.

If you're practicing, you already know how much ACA has cost the medical professional, but it's a lot worse than you might think.

What's a real insult to the medical profession is the Federal Government has reduced physician's income due to new rules, regulations and reduced reimbursements? Even after this, they've increased the Medicare tax on those earning high incomes.

This new income based penalty for Medicare is designed to tax high income earners.

The rationale is those who make more can afford more in taxes.

If physicians are still one of the highest-paid professions, who's affected the most by this new Medicare income based tax and penalty?

You're right, the largest and highest paid profession affected will be physicians. If you're earning more than $250,000, **you may be paying an additional penalty that may near 4%.**

Medicare's not the only tax which will affect you. As I mentioned before, there's **TRIPLE TAX** on Social Security.

The first tax is the 15.3% deducted if you're self-employed. If you're an employee, the cost is 7.65%. This is taken out of your paycheck as soon as you earn it.

The second tax is when these taxes are paid. You don't get a full deduction on the employment part of this tax. This means you're essentially paying tax on the tax.

The third tax is when you retire. If you're eligible for Social Security, you'll pay tax on your Social Security benefits - amazing! I'm assuming you'll pay this triple tax because the only people who get Social Security tax free are those earning under $25,000 for single taxpayers or $33,000 if you're married.

What do you think your tax will cost over your lifetime? Using the average physician's income of approximately $200,000 and the average tax between FICA, federal and state rates of 30%, you'll be paying on average $60,000 per year for your entire working career.

This means, while you might be saving towards a retirement plan, you're actually funding the federal retirement plan called the national budget and deficit.

If all I can do is to show you a few strategies on how to reduce your income tax by only **10%,** that would save you **$6,000** per year.

If you invested that same **$6,000** per year over a thirty year working career at a 6% rate of return, you'll create an extra **$606,438** to your name.

Now, I'll bet that puts a different spin on your motivation to legally reduce your income tax!

CHAPTER 2....
MISTAKE ONE NOT UNDERSTANDING TAX STRATEGIES

If I had a time machine and I could take you back to the mid-1980s when I was a young intern in a multi-disciplined financial planning firm, you would've gotten to see what I would call the Steve Jobs of financial planning.

His name was, William C Moore and he was one of the most intelligent practitioners I've ever met, if not the most intelligent.

He was also one of the country's first true financial planners. He brought tax planners, tax preparers, lawyers, insurance agents, investment managers and financial quarterbacks all under one roof.

During those formidable years I was put through what I would consider a litany of grueling training tasks. Those long hours comprised of preparing taxes, financial plans, investment strategies and estate planning designs.

The firm required every planner to practice each discipline to understand how all the different parts of a person's financial life interconnected.

In the tax area we learned the four cornerstones of tax planning:

1) Deduct
2) Defer
3) Offset
4) Shift

Deducting

You're probably most familiar with tax deductions. This is what your tax preparer goes through with you each year.

Oddly enough, eight out of ten new clients we see aren't missing any tax deductions. This tells us the tax preparers or CPA's are picking up the actual deductions you're allowed.

The problem is, there's eight out of ten of these people in the same group missing out on deferral, shifting and offsetting strategies.

Deferring

You might also be somewhat familiar with deferring. Deferring taxes is usually done through a retirement plan. We're going to cover some of this in Chapter 3.

Don't always believe tax deferral is good. Depending on what tax bracket you're in can determine if it makes sense to defer or not.

Sometimes, physicians will pay more in tax and will lose money because they have the wrong deferral plan set up.

In a recent case, we installed a new type of pension plan in one of our client's offices.

We had to include all of the employees at a net cost of 4.5% of the total contributions. Our client saved 7.65% in FICA taxes by putting these funds away into the retirement plan.

Our client made over 3% per year or over $9,000 a year by putting money away for his employees. This means that this physician is putting away 95.5% of the total plan contributions for himself. The amount he's putting away for his employees does not cost him any money but actually saves him money.
His employees are happy and more productive and our client is saving a ton of taxes.

Offsetting

Offsetting tax is one of the areas a tax planner concentrates on. Deducting and deferring are sometimes touched on by your tax preparer but they almost never cover offsetting.

Look at offsetting like a see-saw. When your income goes up, it's like one end of the see-saw when it goes down.

If your income goes up, your tax bracket goes up too which means your net take home pay goes down.

What's the only way to get the down end of the see-saw to rise? You need to add weight to the other side.

You must have a way to increase deductions which will increase your net pay. The secret is to increase the deductions without physically spending or losing money.

In tax offsetting, we might look at accelerating items which will offset other items.

As an example, you might acquire a mortgage to offset high income.

With your investments, you might book a loss on one investment which would allow a deduction to convert some of your IRA to a ROTH. There are hundreds of strategies that can fall under the tax offset category.

Shifting

Tax shifting is by far the least used strategy.

If you view taxes brackets like buckets, it's easier to visualize.

In your imaginary tax bucket, assume inside there's different levels marked off. These levels denote how full the bucket is. The lowest mark is where the bucket is the least full. The highest mark is where the bucket is the fullest.

The higher the mark, the higher the tax bracket. The more income you pour into the bucket, the higher the level of tax gets, thus filling up your tax bucket.

This is the same way tax brackets work. The higher the income gets, the more you pay in tax on each dollar.

The goal of income shifting is to have as many buckets as legally possible.

27

Your objective is to fill each bucket to the first mark. Once you've filled that bucket to the first mark, move income to a new bucket.

By filling each bucket to the first level you're keeping your average tax bracket low.

You have many different buckets to choose from. Your personal tax return is only one bucket. Maybe you and your spouse could be two buckets, depending on your filing strategy. Your children could provide another bucket. A corporation could be another bucket. A trust could be yet another bucket. An IRA is a bucket. A pension plan is a bucket. An employee benefit plan is also a bucket.

As you can see, there are many buckets you can use to shift your income into.

In certain cases, you might want to fill up one bucket past the first market because there's a tax cap on certain types of taxes.

You also want to make sure that if you pour income into one bucket they don't catch you on secondary taxes.

A secondary tax would be FICA, FUTA, SUTA, NIIT or AMT. These secondary taxes might cause there to be more tax in two buckets as opposed to filling one bucket to a certain level. This strategy works because certain taxes cap out.

An example would be SUTA may only tax you 2.9% on the first $20,000 of income.

Another example may be FICA may only tax you on the first $120,000.

Filling a certain bucket up to a level where the secondary tax is capped but you move the excess to a non-secondary tax bucket can save you taxes.

An example of paying a secondary tax twice is when physicians employ their spouses.

We find physicians commonly get caught paying these secondary taxes such as FICA, FUTA and SUTA taxes when they could be limited. These acronyms stand for Social Security and Medicare, Federal Unemployment and State Unemployment tax.

Depending on when you read this book the limit may be different so I'll explain it in concept.

If you pay a tax rate of say 2% in FUTA on the first $30,000 of income, you would spend $600 per year.

If you pay yourself $50,000 and you pay your spouse $50,000 a year, you're paying the FUTA on both incomes for a total of $1,200.

If you take your spouse off the payroll, you would save one side of the FUTA, or $600 per year. This works with FICA taxes as well.

Throughout the remaining chapters you'll find each one of the tax strategies discussed will fall into one of these four main tax reduction categories.

CHAPTER 3....
MISTAKE TWO TAX
MISTAKES ON
RETIREMENT PLANS

As a physician, you're one of the top earning professions compared to all other professions.

Physicians have lost the first place income earnings position to professional athletes and celebrities. Even with that loss, physicians still count on a very high income.

Obamacare, the government and insurance companies have tried everything they can do to reduce your earnings, yet physicians still earn the highest average income of any service-related profession.

This high income also makes you a target.

The IRS and Congress craft tax laws which look for the deepest pockets to pay off their bad decisions.

You're already a target for high taxes on your income but you're also a target for what you save.

The biggest pot of money that's easy for the government to get their hands on is inside of your retirement plan.

Saving money into a retirement plan has always been one of the most common strategies people think is always the best strategy to save tax.

Unfortunately, tax deferral differs greatly from tax savings.

Maybe I've become cynical in my older age but I view things differently now in my fifties than I used to in my twenties.

As an example, the other day I was waiting to check out at the grocery store. I looked over at the rack of magazines and saw two popular financial magazines.

The first financial magazine's front page said the quickest way to wealth is to max out your 401(k) and retirement plan contributions.

The second magazine's headlines stated that putting the maximum into an IRA is the best thing you could do for your future.

While I might agree it's a good idea to save through a retirement plan if you're a spendthrift, for all the rest, it can be disastrous.

This **"good for all"** financial advice plagues our community and is one of the reasons for our massive financial failing public.

Using this **"good for all"** financial advice would be like saying antibiotics should be given to anyone and everyone who might show a sign of a cold.

One reason I highly disagree with this kind of advice is the goal of a retirement plan. The goal is to put money into the plan when you're in a high tax bracket. The end goal is to withdraw it when you're in a low tax bracket.

The problem is, some of you aren't in the highest tax bracket when you're deferring taxes on your income.

You might be in the middle or lower bracket, yet you're saving the maximum amount into your retirement plan. If this is you, it may come back to bite you when you must take money out of the plan at a higher rate than what you saved by putting it in.

I want you to keep in mind something. Our national deficit is nearing $20 trillion. You need to ask yourself the question, "Who will pay off this debt?"

The reality is the government will need to raise money to pay off their mistakes. They'll do this by taking more money from those people who are *earning* a lot of money or who've *saved* a lot.

If you're in the low to middle tax bracket, there's a high probability you may be deferring $.20 in tax on every dollar deferred but when you're required to take money out, you'll end up paying $.30 or $.40 tax on each dollar.

Instead of saving on taxes, you'll end up paying back more than you've deferred.

Just in case you think you'll "just not take the money out", sorry there's bad news for you.

At age 70 ½ you must start taking the money out. If you don't withdraw your required minimum distribution, there's a 50% penalty on the amount you were required to take.

This concept of not deferring based on your tax bracket might go in direct opposition to most things you read in financial magazines which suggest tax deferral is the greatest thing since sliced bread.

Keep in mind the financial magazines are funded by advertisers and most of those advertisers are mutual fund companies. The motivation for any financial company is to get and keep your funds in their coffers.

By the financial companies convincing you to put as much into retirement plans as possible, they increase their odds they'll hold onto your funds.

Why would a financial company want to try to keep your money in their coffers?

The financial companies make money on your money by a fee or a spread, and sometimes both. If you withdraw money, they'll lose money.

There's a higher chance you'll not withdraw from your retirement plan over your non-retirement plan, if you want or need to spend money due to the taxes and potential penalties from withdrawing from a retirement plan.

If the financial institutions can convince you to put the majority of your money into retirement plans, they'll have a good opportunity of making sure you keep your money invested with them.

This is why a majority of investments recommended by the sales people are mutual funds and variable annuities inside of retirement plans.

Mutual funds are the most expensive way to invest into the equity markets.

As of the writing of this book, the mutual fund market is close to 22 trillion dollars in value. Mutual funds have grown from 600 when I started in practice, to over 31,000.

Mutual funds wouldn't proliferate like rabbits if they weren't extremely profitable.

Anytime advertisements say it's **always** good for **everyone** to put as much as they can into deferred retirement plans, you have a recipe for disaster.

Why is it to your disadvantage to put certain investments into a retirement plan?

When you save money into a retirement plan, you turn any potential of a capital gain tax into an ordinary income tax.

Therefore, you want to strive to pay capital gains tax over an ordinary income tax.

Ordinary income tax is usually 30% to 100% more expensive than the cost of capital gains tax.

As a quick reference, capital gains taxes are put into either a short-term or a long-term category.

A short-term capital gain is any investment held for less than one year.

A long-term capital gain is any investment held for more than one year.

If you sell an investment you've held for less than one year, you'll pay ordinary income taxes on it.

If you hold the investment for longer than one year, you'll get the more preferential tax treatment of a long term capital gain tax rate.

Here's an example based on the 2016 tax rates:

Assumes Married Filing Jointly

Rate	Income
10%	$0-$18,550
15%	$18,550 - $75,300
25%	$75,300 – $151,900
28%	$151,900 - $231,450
33%	$231,450 - $413,350
35%	$413,350 - $466,950
39.6%	$466,950 and above

If you take any money out of your retirement plan, it's accumulated with all your other income.
You'll pay ordinary income tax rates based on the ordinary tax rate schedule which is the highest tax rate.

Compare ordinary income tax rates to capital gains tax rates listed in the tax comparison rate chart:

Tax Bracket	Capital Gain Tax Rate	
	Short Term	Long Term
10%	10%	0%
15%	15%	
25%	25%	15%
28%	28%	
33%	33%	
35%	35%	
39.6%	39.6%	20%

In most cases, an ordinary income tax is

30% to 100% more in tax than a capital gains tax.

You'll hear the sales pitch "funds in a retirement plan are deferred against taxation". This may be true but there'll be a time when you, your spouse or your children will be forced to take the funds out. When the mandatory distributions are forced out, the funds get taxed as ordinary income.

In addition, the income is added to all your other income and causes tax triggers. These tax triggers are increases in other taxes or reductions of deductions.

Why does it make sense for some physicians to pay the tax now versus deferring into a retirement plan?

When you buy a stock, real estate or a business investment outside of a retirement plan there's no tax on the investment unless a dividend is paid or you sell.

If you buy a growth stock, most likely there's no dividend.

If you allow the stock to grow outside the retirement plan, there's no requirement for you to sell it.

Only if you sell, will you pay the capital gains tax and you'll not pay the ordinary income tax rate unless it's a short term gain.

In addition, when you pass away, you can leave the stock to a spouse, child or anyone you want - totally income tax free.

As an example, if you invest $10,000 in a stock today and it's worth $1,000,000 at your death, your beneficiary will get what's called a step up in basis on the pass down of the investment.

Whatever the value of the stock is on your date of death is what the new tax basis is for the person that inherits the investment.

On the other hand, if you've invested in the same stock through a retirement plan, the outcome is quite different. Your $1,000,000 is now 100% income taxable to the person who inherits it.

Remember, there's no step up in basis benefit available on a retirement plan.

Historically, people invested into equities in their retirement plans as their primary strategy. This comes from the concept to put the higher growth investments into the deferred account. This isn't a smart way to allocate investments for tax efficiency.

You put the investments which would normally incur ordinary income tax into the retirement plan.

Put investments which would qualify as a capital gain investment into the non-retirement plan accounts.

Also, look to see if the amount you're saving to your retirement plan, plus interest, will create a large mandatory withdrawal. If it does, it means the retirement plan itself may increase your tax brackets.

The question I always get is, "How do you figure out if I should save money before or after tax?"

The answer is, you must use a sophisticated tool to make these complicated tax projections. You should also run stress tests which would allow you to see what happens if you pay the tax now versus deferring the tax.

A comparison of before and after tax investing and trigger tax analysis needs to be completed.

Once you have completed a side by side comparison you still need to look at all the different angels.

Will you end up having to withdraw money at a higher rate when you could pay the tax now at a lower rate?

41

Will a large annual mandatory distribution cause penalties and trigger taxes?

If you prematurely pass away, what does the tax outcome look like to your spouse or children?

Remember, you must start taking funds out at age 70 ½ and it's all taxable income.

The magical age of 70 ½ has caused many people heartaches when they realize how much they must pay in taxes on what they thought was a tax-advantaged plan.

We've discussed the potential risks and adverse consequences of putting away too much money before tax. Now let's look at those physicians in the high tax bracket.

If you're in the high tax bracket, you might not be maximizing the right type of retirement plan.

Specialized plans might save you on the difference between the bracket you're in now and your bracket you'll be in when you're required to withdraw.

Plans of this nature vary but now there's new developments in retirement plan laws which might allow someone to save up to $300,000 per year.

Structures called Cash Balance Plans also allow you to eliminate the 15.3% FICA tax on your contributions.

Besides the Cash Balance Plan, there's also 412(e)3 plans. These unique plans are making a strong comeback due to recent IRS rule changes.

As I explain these two plans, please understand there are more plan types and combinations that could be right for you which I can't fit into this book.

If you've saved into a 401(k) it's federally income tax deferred but you're still paying either 15.3% FICA tax if you're the employer or the 7.65% tax if you're the employee. The FICA tax still amounts to a substantial amount of money over any period of time.

Let's start with the Cash Balance Plan. To give you the best example, I'll use a real life case. I'll change the names to protect the confidentiality of the physician and the medical practice.

This is a single physician medical practice with ten employees, including the physician.

When I first met her, there wasn't a retirement plan in place. When I asked her why, she said she was already paying everyone top dollar and didn't feel it was fair to put more money into their pockets and less in hers.

She did however share her main concern. She was 58 years old and only amassed a small retirement account of about $500,000.

She told me she felt like she was burning out and knew at best she had another ten years of working.

In the past fifteen years, she put everything into her practice with the building, buying the equipment and marketing. The way this was done is an entirely different discussion, but at least at this point she was netting about $900,000 a year from her practice.

As you can already imagine, she was feeling the pain with the amount of tax she way paying.

After you take all the taxes out, she was losing about 51% of her total gross income. This meant she was netting about $450,000 of income a year.

Between paying for her new house, three children's college, and a second home, she didn't think she had any money left over to save.

If you're a mathematician, you've already figured it out. There's no way she could retire in ten years on her current path.

To replace her current income of $450,000, she'll need about eight million dollars. This assumes she retires at 68 and needs money for at least twenty years at an inflation rate of 3.7%.

This needed number of eight million dollars also assumes she doesn't want to leave any inheritance to her children. She would need all those funds to spend down over time to support her cash flow.

How do you remedy a situation like this? It's difficult, especially when someone gets used to a certain lifestyle. All you can do is to buffer it the best you can.

In our discussion's she made it clear she wasn't willing to give up her home, her children's college or her second home. With all those conditions, here's what we had to do.

We recommended she set up what we refer to as a three-point retirement plan.

The three points are a cash balance plan, a 401(k) and a profit-sharing plan.

At her age she's eligible to put away $255,000 a year.

To sock away this much before tax she would also be required to contribute about $14,000 a year to her employees plans. This accounted for about 5% plus she'd be putting funds into other people's plans.

The catch with this type of planning is when you consider the NIIT tax, (NIIT TAX is the new Net Investment Income Tax created to help fund Obamacare) the taxes on her payroll, her employee's payroll taxes, the federal and the state income taxes, her net out-of-pocket contribution was only about $125,000 a year.

While this won't project to give her the eight million dollars she needs in ten years, it will, with conservative returns, get her close to $3,500,000.

While not the perfect solution, she still must make some concessions to retire in ten years.

The point is, she didn't set these plans up in the past because she wasn't aware of the way to design them properly. She thought she'd have to put more money into the employee's pockets than her own.

When these plans are designed correctly, sometimes it can save you more in tax than what you must put into the employee contributions.

What about the 412(e)3? This plan's been around for many years but it was taken off the market for several years. The reason, in the mid-1990's, insurance sales people abused the idea. The IRS later disallowed the base 412 type of plan.

In recent years, insurance companies have rebooted this plan but have made the rules stricter to comply with the new IRS guidelines.

To best explain how this plan works I'll use another example.

This example has to do with an orthopedic surgeon who was referred to us by his trust lawyer.

In his particular case, he owned shares in a partnership/corporation layer. This means he has his own corporation which he works for.

His corporation sells their services to a general partnership which is comprised of over twenty physicians.

Each physician shares staff, offices, equipment etc. The general partnership collects all the funds for the physicians and pays each physician as an independent contractor.

Some of these physicians are paid as sole proprietors and some through their self-established corporations.

The key problem, he was netting about $800,000 a year through his S corporation.

He tried to reduce his tax by maxing contributions to his SEP retirement plan. This plan only allowed a deduction of about $50,000 a year which didn't make a dent against $800,000 in taxable income.

He also had expenses incurred through the S corporation he couldn't deduct. Two of those expenses were life insurance and long term care insurance. He was spending $20,000 a year for his life insurance and $6,000 a year for his long-term care insurance.

Due to his income, the long-term care insurance was not deductible and normally, life insurance is never deductible.

To understand how we improved his tax situation and total cash flow we first must understand how a 412 (e)3 plan differs from a normal retirement plan.

A 412(e)3 plan allows you to use accelerated cash value life insurance as part of your funding asset for the pension plan.

Due to his age, he was eligible to put away $265,000 a year before tax with no Federal, State or FICA taxes.

In his particular case he didn't have any employees. This was a benefit to him as he wasn't responsible for adding funds to other people's accounts.

When the life insurance was established as a part of the 412 (e)3 plan we used a company which gave him $1,250,000 of life insurance benefit. This life insurance also had an accelerated long-term care rider on it. This means if he becomes disabled, he'll have the use of the death benefit while he's alive.

We used the pension plan to provide the life and long-term care insurance. This allowed us to cancel his personally owned life and long-term care policies.

His old life policy was $750,000 and now he has a new one for $1,250,000.

His old long-term care policy covered him up to a maximum of $455,000. He now has a total death benefit of $1,250,000 which covers him for either life insurance or long-term care insurance.

In summary, this plan has saved him $26,000 a year he was spending on his old life and long-term care premiums.

It also has saved him 45% in Federal, State and FICA taxes on the $265,000.

The net savings each year is over $140,000.

How do you really know if you should be saving into a retirement plan? Which type of plan should you use? How much should you save?

I'll go back to what I call the three rules of planning:

1) Calculate
2) Calculate
3) Calculate

I don't believe it's ever a good idea to *just* take any financial advisors' _opinion._ This is especially true when deciding how much to save before or after tax.

Mathematical calculations must be done to figure out what's best in your particular situation.

Unfortunately, the general financial salesperson and main stream financial media sells well but misleads millions.

If you're a physician and you're not self-employed but you're allowed to put into your 401(k) at work, I suggest you still do the calculations. Figure out if you should put away income into these plans or not.

I want to mention one small note which should always be considered. If you have a 401(k) or company-sponsored plan and they're willing to match you on a certain percentage of your contribution, I would suggest at least investing that percentage.

As an example, if your company matches on the first 3% you put in, you're making a 100% return on your money, day one. No matter what the tax is, you'll still be ahead!

If your investing into a before tax plan without a match and you're in the middle to low tax bracket, you could be depriving yourself of a much better retirement.

Please understand, if you don't have the discipline to invest on your own, then saving into these forced savings programs may be the best thing for you.

Recently a physician came into our office with his wife and they hired us to do these calculations.

They'd been maxing out their retirement plans at over $300,000 per year for the last 12 years.

They at least were putting these funds into the right type of retirement plan by using a defined benefit type.

This type of plan saved them the FICA tax which is a 15.3% return.

Unfortunately, and fortunately their money has grown at a nice rate of return.

They're sitting on close to $8 million in their retirement plans. When you compute a 4%, first year required minimum distribution at age 70 ½, with a modest growth from their current age, the calculations showed they would have over $480,000 in their first year Required Minimum Distribution.

We further calculated if they reduced the amount they're contributing into their current retirement plan by 50%, they'd still save the base Social Security tax but it would save them 2% in income taxes per year at required minimum distribution age.

<u>Two percent (2%) per year on close to $500,000 a year of distributions equates to close to $10,000 per year in tax savings.</u>

While this may not seem like a lot of money, it could pay for a lease payment on a brand-new Mercedes.

Also, in my humble opinion, it would be a nice charitable deduction. By reducing taxes this way, you can decide which charity you give money to. If you don't make this election, you give to the forced charity named the Internal Revenue Service.

The key to understanding the right action is by doing the calculations. These calculations are not to be taken lightly and I warn people against going online and using the free calculators.

Most of these free calculators don't have the complex projection capability built in to give accurate results. After all, a Polaroid picture is not the same as an MRI scan.

Two of the most important tools we use in our practice are MoneyGuidePro and Emoney. Like an expensive MRI, CAT scan or PET scan machine, these financial engineering tools are very expensive but necessary.

If you're already working with a true financial planner or a fiduciary advisor, most likely they'll have access to these tools and can run the heavy calculations for you.

CHAPTER 4....
MISTAKE THREE NOT CREATING A TAX EFFICIENT EXIT STRATEGY

As a physician, you probably started your education with the idea of working for a hospital, then opening your own practice. Unfortunately, times have changed.

For many physicians, they've had to leave their practice, close their practice or sell their practice to go back to work in either a group or employment setting.

Between the costs of employees, malpractice insurance and business operations, it's almost impossible to go it alone.

If you're a physician now, the reasons for the income and financial decline are quite obvious.

- Obamacare
- Medicare
- Insurance companies
- Increased regulations
- Compliance
- HIPPA
- Document Management

With all these changes, the future looks very different for anyone in the medical field.

These changes can also create a problem with the eventual exit strategy for physicians already owning their own practice.

Many physicians don't consider income and capital gains taxes may take back 30% to 50% of the sale of their practice.

In addition, the payout of employee pension plans and sale settlements can also take a large portion of the eventual equity sale.

Hopefully, your goal is to build a successful practice which has value and one day you'll sell the asset to enjoy the rest of your life.

One of the keys to a successful exit strategy is planning a minimum of five to six years in advance.

A comprehensive study of the multiple buyout ratios and metrics of your practice can also improve your selling price.

The number of patients, types of patients, gross revenue per patient, net income per patient, staff and overhead load are all important metrics to understand, far in advance of the sale.

If you understand what these' metrics need to be, you can hire practice management experts to help you reach your targets.

Part of your plan to exit should also be how to sell and minimize your taxation.

If you serve two thousand patients and you're a general practitioner vs. a dermatologist, the practices are valued at opposite ends of the scale.

While a thoracic surgeon or an orthopedic surgeon have much higher annual incomes, they also don't have the same cash flows which can be sold the same as an arthritis specialist.

Each practice is designed differently and has a different expected profit margin and valuation. The key is to understand what your specialization will bring if you want to sell.

When you set the target date to sell, you must also consider the way you're going to get paid and how it will affect your cash flows for your eventual retirement.

Will you get a lump sum and be subjected to capital gains taxes?

Will you take a structured sale and take a down payment with a timed payback?

Depending on your specialization, your personal tax situation and what you need to live on should dictate the structure of your sale.

If you sell the wrong way, you may end up giving back more than fifty percent of the sale price in taxes.

Let's say your practice is grossing $5,000,000 a year. Your net profit is 30% or $1,500,000 to you.

Assuming we used a general valuation and pegged your selling price at $3,000,000 or two times net income, you'll have to pay taxes on either all or a portion of this $3,000,000.

There's other considerations than just the immediate tax. Typically, these types of sales will require you stay around for six months to a year to transition the new owners.

You might be also merging into a group and will continue to work. Each sale and transaction is different.

In either case, your structure will most likely be a combination of salary and capital gains for the patient list.

The taxes depend on how the income is classified. Depending on the accounting, you could pay a recapture of depreciation on equipment if your practice bought the equipment.

Later on you'll learn why a separate entity to hold equipment may make sense for not only asset protection and current tax benefits but also to avoid the recapture of the depreciation.

When it's time to sell, it's too late to start to figure out a tax exit strategy.

If you're able to create a strategy in advance, there's a few different methodologies which can be used to reduce or in some cases eliminate the tax.

One of those strategies is to utilize what's referred to as a 453 trust. If structured correctly, this trust allows the sale of the practice and either deferral or complete elimination of the capital gains taxation.

The upside to the 453 trust is the assets you receive from the sale of your practice can also have total asset protection.

Let's go back to the example of selling the practice for $3,000,000. In this example we're going to assume any equipment you're selling has been put into its own LLC or corporation.

When you sell, you can continue to lease the equipment to the new owners or you can close the corporation down.

In either case we'll assume the recapture of the depreciation is not a part of the sale for the $3,000,000 example.

Included in $3,000,000 is a salary portion. You'll agree to stay on for one year for a salary of $250,000 to transition staff and patients to the new owners.

This $250,000 is going to be taxed to you as ordinary income. If you've set up a consulting company, the buyers can pay this consulting company. The buyer gets the normal income tax deduction on the $250,000 but now you can segregate the income into a separate tax bucket.

This will leave $2,500,000 in the form of a capital gain.

To make this example easier we'll assume the buyer writes you a check and there's no timed payment.

Let's make one more assumption for ease of understanding. There's zero basis in the business and the entire $2,500,000 is taxable.

What you'll want to do is far prior to the sale (at least one year) is to set up a Deferred Gains Trust. This is also referred to as a 453 trust.

This trust must be set up by a non-related grantor such as a friend or non-lineal relative. You must also find a trustee that's not a relative. These two parties will set up the trust. Last, you can name your children as the eventual beneficiaries. If you don't have children, you can name anyone you want as the eventual recipients of the trust after your die. This can be done by directly naming them or you can name a trust on their behalf.

Once this non-grantor-related trust is set up, you'll either do an asset sale or a stock sale. Most likely you'll do an asset sale.

This means you'll sell the patient list, the staff and the records. In a stock sale which is rare, you'll sell the actual stock of your company.

(The reason this sale is rare is buyers don't want your liabilities that come with your company. Mostly, they're only interested in the patients' cash flow and the trained staff).

You're going to sell either the assets or the stock to the 453 trust. The trustee of the 453 trust buys your stock or assets for the fair market value. This fair market value is, in our example $2,500,000.

Your trust doesn't have any money for the purchase so how will they buy this from you?

You're going to allow them to borrow the money from you. In short, you're going to hold a note for the $2,500,000.

The trustee of the trust sells your assets to the buyer and receives the cash. The trustee invests those monies to produce an income. This income is how the note gets paid back to you.

The question now becomes; how much tax do you owe?

Nothing, you didn't receive anything of value so you don't owe any tax?

The next question is when will you pay the tax?

The tax due all depends on how you negotiate the note with the trustee. If the note is an interest only note, you'll only pay tax on the interest income as you receive it.

If your note is an amortized note, you pay tax on it in two parts. You'll first pay tax on the interest received at ordinary income tax rates. The principal portion of the payback is taxed as a capital gain.

Let's consider a different scenario. If we used an example where your basis (basis is the cost of your investment) is one half of the sale price, you'll have three parts paid back to you in the note payment.

The first part is the interest which is taxed as ordinary income tax, just like the last example.

The second part is the capital gain portion which would be fifty percent of the principal repayment portion (due to you having a 50% basis allocation in the sale) and this portion is taxed at the more preferable capital gains tax rates.

Finally, the third portion is the other half of the principal part of the payment. This is tax-free as it's considered a payback of your basis.

Here's an example and comparison of the two methods of selling your practice.

Example 1

The straight sale method.

Sale Price $3,000,000
Salary Portion $250,000
Tax on Salary   45%
(Assumes Federal and FICA taxes.)

Salary tax cost $112,500

$2,500,000 taxed at capital gains tax rates
(20% + 3.8% NIIT = 23.8%)

$595,000 Capital Gains Tax

Total Tax $707,500
(Tax on salary plus the capital gains tax)
Net to you $2,292,500

If you invested this money at a 6% rate of return, you would receive $137,550 in annual income before tax.

Example 2

Use a DGT / 453

Gross Sale $3,000,000
*$250,000 goes to your consulting company
*(Taxed at 20% total or $50,000)

$2,500,000 is sold to your trust and you hold back a note at 6%.

Total taxes paid would be $50,000

Net invested at 6% = $177,000 a year.
Almost a $40,000 increase in annual income.

In the above example I'm using 6% for the note the trust owes you.

A DGT/453 can, in most cases, increase your net after tax income.

I've used the sale of your practice as the example here, but this device can be used for real estate and or stock. If as an example you also owned the medical building, and you included this in the sale you could either use the same 453 trust or set up a second trust to set up different terms.

One of the biggest questions I get is "What is my liquidity with the money in the trust?"

Remember, you hold a note with the trustee being the borrower and you're the lender. This note can have a pay on demand feature. If it does, it means you have liquidity. It also means if you demand part or all of the note from the trust for liquidity you'll pay the capital gains taxes on it.

The key to remember is this device works because you don't take constructive control or receipt of the gain. When you do, you pay the tax.

There's other uses for this type of trust in multi-generational estate planning and in asset protection planning.

Depending on your discipline and your state, you have a liability tail. This is the time limit someone can come after you for a malpractice suit. These types of devices can be used to protect assets and income.

In today's litigious environment, the average American is sued 3.3 times during their lifetime. While we don't have hard statistics for physician's we know they're the largest targets for lawsuits today.

For physicians, their risk isn't always from patients, but from employees as well.

The growing risk of employment labor law increases your chances of losing income and assets to a frivolous employment lawsuit.

Due to this tax and asset protection aspect we've seen an increase in the use of these types of trusts.

Another strategy to mitigate or reduce the tax is to use employee stock option plans. These allow a transfer of stock at a reduced tax over time. This is a unique strategy and must be handled carefully because it depends upon the type of medical practice and the makeup of employees.

You can structure these plans as Phantom Stock Agreements, an ESOP or even a Restricted Stock Plan.

The advantages are if you're in a multi-discipline practice or a multi-partner practice, they'll allow the purchase of company stock by the employees or a grant of stock by the owners. The plans allow more of a transition to partners or employees as an exit strategy.

Another common strategy we use to help a physician's exit is either a section 1202 or 1244 stock strategy.

These are like many plans we discuss. They're available to every physician but not usually talked about by the accounting community.

There are many plans and strategies which aren't recommended because of misunderstandings by accountants. One of those is the C Corporation.

I'll cover these in more detail but for now the benefit of the C corporation is it has its own tax bracket.

The problem is if there's a profit in the corporation and its paid out as a dividend, the dividend isn't deductible to the corporation but its taxable to the stockholder. This creates double taxation since the corporation paid taxes on the income and the individual pays it again.

If you have a C corporation we don't ever want to pay out a dividend. We'll want to hold the profit inside the corporation as a retained earnings instead of paying it out as a dividend.

The IRS has a limit of the amount you can retain of about $250,000. Keep in mind, you're allowed an unlimited amount in retained earnings. You must however keep a documented plan on how you're going to use the money. It must be allocated for business expansion or business purposes.

You can retire and keep your corporation going to pay for expenses even if you sell the assets as I explained in the sale example prior.

This strategy is allowed as long as you still have legitimate business operations. Public speaking or consulting are legitimate business operations, especially for physicians. You can even convert this corporation to a real estate investment company.

If you've set up this company and plan on keeping it into retirement, you'll need a good plan.

In order for you to use the retained earnings and get all the benefits, you need to be very careful to structure your income and expenses after you sell your practice. You may have more expenses than you have in annual revenues which means the corporation will show a loss each year. Each year you show the loss, it reduces the retained earnings. You can even get to a point where you're adding in funds to the corporation to continue to fund your consulting or your public speaking.

This strategy can be used if you expect a large capital gain in other parts of your financial life. You can later close the company down and take a capital loss.

There's other benefits with this structure. Let's also assume that during retirement you're paying for what would not be deductible by you personally.

What might those expenses be?

Your health insurance or medical costs. As an individual, typically you'll not be able to deduct these costs. The reason is you'll first have to exceed ten percent of your adjusted gross income before you can deduct dollar one of medical costs.

In this strategy you'll continue to pay for these expenses until there's no more business operations.

When your business operations cease, we're assuming you've run down your retained earnings and run up large losses for the corporation.

If you have losses, then close the corporation down and claim a 1244 loss. The beauty of this election is you can take an ordinary loss against other income.

There is one caveat on structuring a 1244 election. Normally we create a revocable living trust for a person. We put your company stock into this trust for probate and health care protection. Under 1244, it doesn't allow the loss for a trust. The rules are vague so it's safer to transfer the company stock prior to the close down and save questions from the IRS.

If there's a period of time between the transfer of stock back to you and the close down, make sure you have a pour over will and an up to date Durable Power of Attorney.

Again, these strategies are important to be planned at least 3 to 5 years in advance. If they're done correctly, they can mitigate, reduce or potentially eliminate the tax on the sale.

Lastly, there's the long-term buyout strategy of bringing in an apprentice or a younger physician. This can be tax efficient but poses its own set of issues and problems.

I want to make sure you don't try the duck and transfer strategy. This has been tried and although in some cases it's worked successfully, I still would not suggest it.

This duck and transfer strategy is where you bring in a younger physician or even one of your children to your practice.

We're had a lot of clients where their children become physicians. They're goal is to pass the practice down to them without taxation.

In this duck and transfer strategy you try to bring in the related party and they magically take over.

There's not a formal sale or transfer of stock for tax purposes but an attempt to transfer the company without taxation.

Many physicians have tried this and asked me to facilitate this transfer. The reason I won't do it is it's clearly not allowed.

Whenever you bring in family or a related party you are scrutinized by the IRS even more than normal.

This isn't to say you can't sell to a family member, it means it's better to have an arm's length transaction.

There's other ways to grant, gift and even transfer ownership of your practice to a related party.

These methods are called discounted share methods. These requires the setup of trusts; family limited partnerships or entities you can insert outside parties in control. Once you complete this, then you can apply what's called a lack of control or lack of market discount.

If your practice is worth $3,000,000 to the general medical market, you could sell it in a tax efficient method to your relative for approximately 70% of the taxable value.

This is a considerable tax advantage, especially if you use a note, like explained with the 453 trust.

There's not one perfect way to create a tax efficient exit strategy. All strategies should be considered and a planner should be employed to run through the "what if" scenarios and future tax projections.

The planner or consultant you hire should be investing in the top end tools that can simulate different selling metrics and methods to determine the best outcome.

These "what-if" scenarios should be presented and explained to you. Please don't just take an opinion or a guess from someone. Get the calculations done and redone each year to make sure you're on the right track.

As with any successful outcome, you must have a plan in place.

You've heard the saying that "a successful exit starts with a well-planned beginning."

Most people don't plan to fail, they fail to plan!

The problems we've seen are when physicians and partners of medical partnerships take advice from someone that's just looking at their current legal or financial structure but failing to look into the future.

It could also be an accountant that's only looking at their current tax structure but failing to compute different combinations of future outcomes based on strategies.

This lack of forward looking is no different than trying to walk forward by always looking down at your toes.

You must look ahead and understand where you want to go. This then dictates the type of entities and tax structure you'll need to have in place.

CHAPTER 5....
MISTAKE FOUR
USING THE WRONG
TYPE OF COMPANIES

As I previously stated, "to move forward you must **look forward** and not down at your feet, otherwise you'll trip".

Using the wrong type of company or entity structure is a common problem we see.

The traditional way a physician starts their medical practice is through a sole proprietorship. This method is thought of as the simplest way but usually ends up being the most tax expensive way.

The reason it's the most popular way physicians start off in practice is because it's easy and inexpensive to set up a sole proprietorship.

Once the physician starts to make money the usual recommendation is to change to an S Corporation.

Twenty to thirty years ago, S Corporations became the most popular entity of choice for physician's offices.

We've found most accountants today recommend their physician clients run their practices through either a sole proprietorship or an S Corporation.

In a recent case, a very successful pediatrician hired us for a tax plan. The first thing that jumped out at me was he was still using a sole proprietor as his business filing.

This is where you file a schedule C and all income and expenses flow through to you individually. To bring back a previous lesson, it's where you fill up one single tax bucket.

The problem with his case is he was netting over $750,000 a year. This income was fully taxed at FICA tax rates along with all his income being funneled into his person returns. Again, all income is going into one tax bucket.

Once you get over a certain amount of income, you'll receive tax penalties for earning too much.

Here's a small list of the penalties:

1) Medicare excise tax
2) NIIT Tax
3) Alternative Minimum Tax
4) Reduction or loss of your medical, mortgage, property tax and charitable deductions.
5) Increase in the net tax bracket

I could go on and on but I'm sure you get the idea. If you're putting all your income on the same tax return, you'll most likely encounter some of these same costs.

I'm still seeing physician's making $300,000 to $500,000 a year operating under a sole proprietorship or just an S Corp. The problem with both entity structures is they operate under the American Tax Funnel.

The American Tax Funnel is where all your income gets funneled into one place, which is your personal 1040 tax return. All your income stacks on top of itself and increases your tax brackets, increases your tax triggers and adds up to be one of the highest ways to pay taxes. In simple terms it's pouring all your income into one bucket.

An S Corporation contributes to the problem of the American Tax Funnel because it pushes all your net income onto your personal tax return. It does however do one thing a sole proprietor cannot do. It can limit the amount of FICA taxes you're paying.

In a sole proprietor filing, 100% of all of your income is FICA taxed at the current 7.65% (Up to the FICA Limit) for the employee and 7.65% to the employer for a total of 15.3%, (You do get a deduction on the self-employment side of the payment). If you're making $200,000 a year, you'll pay between $15,000 and $20,000 for your FICA taxes.

By running your business through an S Corporation you can split the income between salary and what I'll call a dividend. Technically, this distribution isn't a dividend but most people understand what a dividend means so we'll use that vernacular.

Let's assume you own 100% of the stock of an S Corporation. Let's also assume your practice makes $500,000.

If you're paying yourself $100,000 in wages, you're paying FICA taxes on this $100,000. You'll have $400,000 left over which is not classified as wages.

As the shareholder you'll get a distribution of $400,000. This comes to you in the form of a K1 distribution. The difference with this method is you don't pay the full FICA taxes on the dividend. You're only paying the FICA taxes on the wage portion.

Years ago an S Corporation was the perfect solution to split income between wages and a dividend thus saving taxes on FICA.

Now the IRS has new rules which reduce this netting strategy. These new taxes and limits are the net investment income tax and reasonable comparison salaries rule. Sometimes, it may end up costing you more to pay yourself this way than in prior years.

You may save on the total FICA tax but an S Corporation will not save any Federal or State income tax. It's still funneled through your 1040 tax return. Again, it's like pouring all your income into one bucket.

One last caveat, don't underpay yourself for your services. While there's room for interpretation, if the salary can't be justified, don't do it.

As an example, don't say you're only making $25,000 in salary and earning $475,000 in a distribution.

Another issue is when I see a physician putting their spouse on the payroll. Most times the cost to put the spouse on payroll far outweighs any Social Security benefit or any benefit to a retirement plan contribution.

With Social Security, the spouse is entitled to one half of your benefit or their own, whichever is more. This is the case whether they are getting a salary or not.

In a majority of the cases, the benefit to the spouse by being under your Social Security is higher than if they tried to claim their own benefit.

This means it's a complete waste of money for the spouse to be paying into Social Security.

The strategies we just reviewed would be under the strategy of tax shifting.

Another way of reducing income tax is tax splitting. This is where, if you have the legal authority to justify it, you can split your income into different entities and different tax brackets.

Going back to the buckets again, it's like having multiple buckets and only filling up each bucket to a certain level.

As an example, if you own your medical building, you can create a separate entity which manages the property. This entity could be a regular C Corporation.

Rental income from your building would be paid into the separate tax entity. The rent is paid by your medical practice. This separate tax entity will have its own set of books and its own deductions.

You may have been given the common warning from some accountants, "Never set up a C Corporation because it will cause double taxation." This is one of the most ridiculous warnings I've heard over and over again.

This advice usually comes from a tax person who does not understand how to avoid double taxation on a C Corp.

You would only pay double taxation if you paid out a dividend. A dividend is only mandated when you've reached an excess of retained earnings.

The government usually puts this limit at about $250,000. There is however an exemption on these maximum retained earnings.

If you can prove you have a legitimate business purpose for holding onto retained earnings, you have an unlimited amount that you can retain.

In addition, you can invest those retained earnings within the corporation for future business use.

If the corporation is run and structured correctly, you should never have the demand to pay out a dividend and thus be subjected to a double taxation.

What if you want to sell your practice like we discussed in Chapter 4?

Once you sell your medical practice, hopefully you've structured the right type of entity. If so, you can also continue using this entity as long as you have a business purpose.

In many cases, our physician clients sell their medical practices and they continue to hold their medical license and or lecture to earn income. This is one of the best setups for retirement.

If it's structured correctly, any of the retained earnings sitting inside these entities can be spent down on ordinary business expenses otherwise known as Section 162 expenses.

These companies are referred to as a Physician's Retirement Company. It's a company that when set up correctly can hold assets of your medical practice. The company may even retain some of the sale earnings once you exit full-time practice. It allows you to continue operating as a physician, a speaker or any type of business and still use some of those assets for normal and ordinary business expenses.

Normal and ordinary business expenses are called Section 162 expenses. Expenses that qualify may be travel, automobile, retirement plans, medical insurance, medical reimbursement plans, reimbursement, use of an office in the home, cell phone and many other expenses which are reasonable and ordinary business expenses.

Today, you have unlimited creativity between the structure of your business entities and tax flow.

You can use:

- Trusts
- LLC's taxed as an S Corp
- LLC's taxed as disregarded entities
- LLC's taxed as C Corporations
- C Corporations

Corporations may be structured to allow different taxpayers to utilize each companies' benefits. You may own one type of company and your spouse or children may own a different type. You want to take advantage of all the benefits of each type of corporation.

It may seem like some of these ideas are in the gray area, they're not. They're all acceptable and normal tax strategies. You must however follow the rules and make sure you keep good records.

Just because someone hasn't told you about strategies like these doesn't make them illegal.

If you've not been told about these ideas, it's more likely the present person doing your taxes either isn't aware of them or they're too busy to calculate if they'll work for you.

Sometimes tax people scare people into not utilizing a strategy with fear of an IRS audit. This tactic is usually due to the tax person not understanding the strategy or covering up their inability to understand or set up these strategies.

Sometimes, I'm asked to do things that go outside the law. I don't do it! You don't need to even consider going outside the law. There're plenty of legal tax strategies to reduce your tax.

CHAPTER 6....
MISTAKE FIVE
BUSINESS TAX
MISTAKES

Financial mistakes are sometimes made when physicians buy equipment, set up retirement plans or set up health or benefit plans for employees.

Let's start with equipment purchases.

J Paul Getty said it the best:

"That which appreciates-purchase, that which depreciates- rent."

Equipment Purchases

I've seen many physicians make the choice to purchase equipment because they don't want debt.

If you have the right entity structure, it can limit your liability, reduce your overall costs and save taxes.

Such equipment purchases can be bought inside a limited liability company and you may get more benefits than buying inside of your primary medical company.

Depending on the structure, you can also lease back equipment to your business. At the end of the lease you can buy the equipment. You can then make a decision to upgrade the equipment or even lease it to other medical offices.

I've also see a lot of mistakes when deducting depreciation. Most of these mistakes are because of a culture, belief system or bad habits from the person preparing the tax returns.

I've always taken the outlook, a bird in the hand is better than five in the bush.

If you buy a piece of equipment, you want to get a section 179 deduction. This depreciation method allows up to a 100% deduction of the depreciation in the first year.

Depending on how you structure your entities and the income into each one, you may be able to buy more equipment and extend your section 179 deduction more than the limit for one person or entity.

This deduction allows you to take either all or most of the deduction in the first year of purchase.

Most times, depending on the equipment, it must be depreciated between five and fifteen years.

I've asked certain accountants why they would purposely choose to depreciate something over a long period vs. the one time, up front deduction.

Here's what I've heard from some accountants:

- That is the way I've always done it.
- I want to keep all equipment depreciation schedules uniform for ease of preparing the tax returns.
- I get to charge the client for preparation of the depreciation schedules every year.
- What's the difference?

Whatever the reason might be, the bottom line is, get your deduction now. The future value of money in your hand is better than in the hands of the IRS.

Retirement Plans

Most retirement plans are sold, not bought.

In a recent case, the client asked us to do an analysis of a plan they were proposed with by a 401(k) salesperson.

This salesperson was from one of the major insurance companies. Like most of these salespeople, they're told what to sell. What they're usually told to sell has the highest profit margins for the insurance company or the largest commissions for the salesperson.

My attitude has always been if I buy a financial product with the highest profit margin for the financial company or salesperson, it means I'm getting the short end of the stick.

First, let's review what the salesperson proposed.

The physician was fifty-five years old. He was making $300,000 net income from his practice with four employees.

The proposed 401(k) would allow him to put away about $23,000 a year, tax deferred. In addition to his own contributions he would need to contribute about $4,000 to his employee's accounts. He would also incur an annual administration cost of about $2,000.

What the sales person didn't explain was the doctor would have to pay full FICA taxes at a 15.3% rate on the 401(k) contributions. This additional expense would apply to his personal deferrals but also to his employee's contributions.

When this physician originally hired us it was only for a second opinion on the 401-K. We discovered a few financial facts at our initial interview so we did a full financial plan.

During this planning process we found he was paying $6,000 a year for his personal life insurance. The premiums were being paid for with after-tax dollars. The net before tax cost to the physician was $9,000.

We compared the original proposal against using a mix of a Cash Balance Plan, 401(k), a profit-sharing plan and finally a 412(e)3 plan.

We ended up recommending the 412(e)3 plan. Using this type of plan, he could cancel his life insurance and pay for a new life insurance policy through the 412(e)3 plan with before-tax dollars.

He would reduce his annual administration fee from $2,000 a year to $500 a year and could save up to $120,000 a year as opposed to the $23,000 a year.

Finally, he would eliminate the FICA taxes with the 412(e)3 plan. The reason is, the 412(e)3 is deducted without FICA tax.

There's no way to tell what the right combination is for anyone without looking at their total financial fingerprint.

Trying to decide on the right plan from a pitch from a salesperson is like getting medical advice over the phone.

With a medical diagnosis you must see the patient, do the tests and make sure what you're recommending to the patient is based on a balance between science and intuition.

When a salesperson is recommending "their product", they're not seeing all the moving parts.

These moving parts are important as you might make a decision in one area but hurt yourself in another.

Health Benefits

Under Obamacare, you must tread carefully with benefits for employees.

As of July, 2015 you can no longer pay for health insurance premiums with a health reimbursement arrangement.

The penalties are $100 per day per employee for continuing such a practice.

The new rules also put more regulation, reporting and penalties on benefits given to any business owner.

Under the new rules you can, however, use a section 105 plan which has a third-party administrator.

In the typical business structure, you try to deduct health benefit costs for employees under your normal and ordinary business expense category.

The problem is, as the business owner you're more limited to what you can and cannot deduct.

By using an HSA and or a Section 105 plan you can maximize and deduct all your medical expenses if they're set up correctly.

CHAPTER 7....
MISTAKE SIX NOT GETTING THE RIGHT ADVICE

Another one of the big mistakes physicians make is getting advice from the wrong person or company.

This doesn't differ from the problematic physicians found in the medical profession.

Just because someone's able to pass the medical exam, certainly doesn't mean their capable of practicing sound medicine.

How many physicians have you met over the years and asked yourself, "How did they pass the exam?"

Not only that, some doctors who have legitimate licenses should never be allowed to touch a single patient.

This isn't any different in the financial profession. You can pass the BAR exam, the Certified Financial Planner exam or the CPA exam and all this means is this person could remember facts and answer questions to pass the exam.

It doesn't mean they're able to apply any of their test questions to real-life scenarios.

Each professional also requires a certain mental expertise which applies to their discipline.

As an example, an architect has spatial logic whereas an engineer has number logic.

Depending on which discipline in the financial field you're hiring they need the attributes which give them the mental horsepower to think outside the box for you.

At least in the medical world they require a rigorous upfront internship and mentor program. While this may not be perfect, at least it weeds out most of those weak practitioners before they'll have people's lives in their hands.

Unfortunately, in the financial world, someone can pass their Certified Financial Planner exam and still possess no idea on how to put together a financial or tax plan.

I used to think the initials after someone's name gave them the credibility to be experts in their field. I soon learned that I was grossly wrong. How might I know this? I've worked with and even hired many of these people.

These same people didn't very last long because we had to either fire them or they quit under their own accord.

I believe I'm a good judge on the lack of strategies being used because I get to see thousands of people a year. I see firsthand the quality of the tax and financial plans being produced and quite frankly, most are garbage.

When reviewing many of these plans, we find only about one out of fifty are structured accurately.

What a wonderful day it is when I finally see a plan which is correctly engineered and well thought out.

If you're like most of our clients, you've been overrun with propositions from about every financial salesperson in your town.

The question is, whom do you trust? That's a tough question to answer. Many financial headlines are peppered with financial advisors stealing money or losing money for their clients.

How do you find someone you can trust but also can think "outside the box" and deliver tax savings ideas to help you?

Do you find a good advisor through referrals?

93

Do you find a good advisor through a current lawyer?

Do you find a good advisor through the internet?

I wouldn't suggest any of these methods as the way to make your decision on whom to work with.

You can get names this way but a referral or internet search is only the beginning.

The best way to find someone is to know the right questions to ask. Like dealing with someone in the medical field you need to know what questions to ask.

I've developed a list of questions to ask a potential financial planner before you hire them.

Here is what to ask:

1. Who they are. Ask for their personal background.

2. Who do they work for now and whom have they worked for in the past?

3. How they are compensated? Fiduciary, broker or both?

4. What services do I get for the fee? Are there any other charges?

5. Are there connected services such as legal, tax, insurance, and if so, how does the coordination work? Differentiate between them knowing someone and having a team in-house.

6. Review their communication's policy and who would do what. (a communications' policy is a written format of who you work with, how you communicate and what their turnaround time is in getting back to you.) This prevents a situation where you think you're working with one person but then get passed to someone else.

7. Review of their ADV Part II and Firm Brochure.

8. What is their initial process?

9. What is their ongoing process?

10. Who do they specialize with?

11. What is their criteria for being accepted as a client? If they don't do both a financial and a personality test, they'll probably accept anyone. This is a common cause for

frustration as they might only care about taking in assets and new clients, not providing the highest expertise in whom they serve.

12. What actions would be cause to be let go as a client? If they don't have this outlined, I would be wary. It should be clear as to the type of person they want to deal with and why you as a client might be let go.

13. Is there a continuity plan in place in case of disaster? If your documents, taxes, insurances, financial plans are with one person, do they have protections and steps in place to protect you? This could include death; disability or retirement of the person you are working with.

14. Can they share resources to learn what strategies they use?

15. How many clients does the person you're dealing with handle? Each advisor or direct person you deal with should not be working with more than 75 clients. We know this to be a maximum number even with the best tools. When they are operating all the tasks necessary to keep your plan in alignment, this should be the maximum.

16. On average, how much time and how many meetings will it take to get your plan on the right track?

    a. Will the amount of time or meeting schedule change over time? I know in our practice, the first year we spend about forty hours meeting with and working on a new client's plan. In the second year it drops to twenty hours. In the third and subsequent years it only takes about ten hours. This is because initially it takes us a long time to get everything on track. Once we get everything fixed, our technology oversees the direction of the plan. The technology tells us when someone's getting off track so we can look into it. If the plan is set up correctly, the ongoing management is much easier, assuming there's automation tools in place.

17. If there's an automated management system in place to oversee my plan what are the costs? I believe this is the most important question. If you're working with a planner who has over ten clients, there's no way they can be overseeing your investments, taxes, insurances, trusts and overall financial plan on a daily basis. This is where the technology and automation come into play.

These tools are very expensive, which is why many planners set up plans but don't monitor them full time. It's important to know if you're hiring a full-time manager or just someone who will only draw the plan, but not monitor it. Ask to see what and how they actually monitor your total plan. Will they monitor your plan on paper and files or do they have a technology system that will automate it? If they have an automated system, they should be excited to show this to you. If they own an automated system, ask them if they use it for presentation or do they really use it to oversee a plan? We know many advisors will tell clients they oversee and manage their plans but don't. They even own the technology to automate a plan but don't. In order for it to work there needs to be someone dedicated to watching the technology on a daily basis. Many advisors make a great pitch but once they have the client sign, they move onto the next. Really inspect and understand what you're paying for.

I would suggest you initially do the interview by phone or send the questionnaire by email or mail. This way, you can leave the human emotion out of the equation.

I'm changing and improving the questions all the time. If you'd like the most up-to-date questionnaire, you can go to kenhimmler.com/trf and you'll find the most updated, detailed questionnaire on what to ask before you hire such a person.

While this method of questioning is not perfect, it's better than some of the other methods of finding that financial ship captain to guide you through the treacherous seas of your financial future.

In today's confusing financial environment, it makes sense to understand what types of advisors' there are. Today, we can narrow it down to three types of advisors.

The first is called a fiduciary advisor and, the second is called a broker. The third is a combination of the first two. They refer to these advisors as Hybrid Advisors.

A fiduciary advisor is as close to a physician as you'll get in the financial world. They must, above all, put the client's interests first. Under no condition are they allowed to do anything in their own or their company's best interest.

A broker works for themselves and a brokerage company. Their responsibility is to put their company or their company's interests first. The law does not allow a broker to explicitly harm a person with a financial transaction. However, it doesn't require them to put the client's interests above all else like with a fiduciary

There's a fundamental difference between working with a fiduciary and a working with a broker.

What about a Hybrid Broker? The only way I can explain this type of broker is to give you an example.

Imagine a patient came to a doctor whom we'll refer to as a hybrid doctor.

The hybrid doctor has all the best intentions in the world but he receives a payment override or commission on every test the patient takes. He also receives a commission on every prescription the patient is written.

While the Hippocratic Oath may resonate in this physician's brain, could his or her actions be dictated by his wallet?

A hybrid financial advisor, otherwise known as a hybrid broker, carries a series 65 or is registered with both the Securities Exchange Commission and FINRA.

This means in some cases, this person sells financial products and earns a commission and sometimes they work on an hourly or fee basis.

The problem is it's up to the client to fully understand what advice is being given. Is this advisor giving advice under the premise of commission or under a fiduciary responsibility?

Not too long ago I met a physician in my office who was dealing with a large brokerage house.

This physician is very successful in his own business and holds over $10 million in this brokerage companies accounts.

When I explained he was working with a Hybrid Broker, he almost fell off of his chair. He had no idea the brokerage company didn't owe him a fiduciary responsibility.

I met with this client again and he confessed he called the broker after our prior meeting and asked him if he was working with him as a fiduciary or as a broker. The broker said it all depended on what they were doing for him.

This physician was very upset because this was never explained to him in the past.

He further stated he was uncomfortable because he didn't know what type of advice he was getting.

Was the advice given on financial actions motivated by a large commission? Could there have been another action taken which would have been better for him but would have paid this person a much smaller fee?

He told me this one piece of information was the biggest eye opener he'd gained from our first meeting. Now, a lot of the recommendations which were made over the years finally made sense to him.

Why hasn't the government done more about this?

When you have a financial industry controlled by Wall Street, mutual funds and a "good old boy" culture, it will be a long time until positive changes are made.

Unfortunately, the regulations allow brokers to call themselves financial planners, even though they may never put a financial plan together.

This has been frustrating to all of us on the fiduciary side as it would be the same as an x-ray technician being allowed to render medical advice.

The x-ray technician has been trained and can operate the machine but they don't have the expertise or experience of a physician.

An X-Ray tech may not render medical advice but a broker or financial advisor is allowed to act as a financial planner even though they're not.

While I've been focusing on the financial advisors, let's not forget lawyers and CPA's make up a big portion of your financial team.

The best example I can give you on the failure of a lawyer is my own grandfathers situation.

My grandfather died in the mid-70s but he died with a sizable estate. He was a master at accumulation and creating businesses for income but failed at having a good distribution and estate plan.

The problem was he had a terrible estate lawyer. This was the same lawyer that helped him through his corporations and his business dealings but designed one of the worst estate plans I've ever seen.

After my grandfather died, the wealth he'd accumulated was lost in its entirety to taxes, other families and, of course, legal fees.

CPA's are not exempt from this problem. Keep in mind the majority of the CPA exam is on corporate finance, corporate audits and compilations. A smaller part of the CPA exam is given to entity structuring, retirement plans, employment plans, income tax structuring and personal tax planning.

You also have to understand the philosophy of some of the CPA's. A lot of them are indirectly working for the IRS instead of working for you. This happens when the CPA or accountant has an attitude if you make a lot of money it's an honor to pay a lot of tax. Yes, I've actually heard that over the years more times than you can imagine.

Recently, Senator Warren suggested there be a law passed which would require the IRS to prepare peoples tax returns, like they do in Denmark.

Elvis tried this method of the IRS preparing his tax returns. He distrusted accountants so much that he had the IRS do his taxes. In some years he paid 90% in tax. In the end, it wasn't the accountant who ended up stealing from him, it was his friend and manager who ripped him off.

As stated before, my recommendation would be to go to the website and download the financial questionnaire and ask the hard questions of the people you're considering dealing with.

That website is kenhimmler.com/trf

CHAPTER 8....
INCORRECT
INVESTMENT TAX
STRUCTURE
BONUS CHAPTER

By now, you should have a good idea that the amount of tax you pay is controlled by how you structure your tax plan.

It's the same for structuring your investments.

By having the right tax structure around your investments you can afford to take much less risk on your investments because you'll end up netting more.

Let's start off by explaining the basics. There's two types of tax on investments.

The first category of tax is called ordinary income tax. This category of tax hits you with the highest tax rate possible.

The second category is capital gains tax. If an investment is held for less than one year, it's considered a short-term gain. If it's a short term gain, you'll pay ordinary income tax rates. If an investment is held longer than one year, then it's considered a long-term capital gain and it's taxed at a much lesser rate.

As an example, if in 2016 you earn less than $449,000, your capital gains tax rate will be 15%. If you earn greater than $449,000, your capital gains tax rate is 20%.

We'll refer back to some of the information we discussed earlier about the American Tax Funnel. If you remember, this is where all your income pours into the funnel and you ride up the income tax bracket ladder.

In the other example it's like filling up one tax bucket with all your income. In this example the bucket is your personal 1040 tax return.

If your funds are in an ordinary income tax type investment and outside of a retirement account, you're still pouring income into your tax funnel.

Investments like bonds, CDs, REITs, convertibles and high dividend stocks will cause taxation each year.

In these types of investments, you cannot stop or elect to defer the dividend or interest. At the end of the year you'll receive a 1099 or a K-1 which reports your dividends, interest or distributions.

Even if you don't need the dividend or distribution you'll still pay the tax on it.

In my book titled Live Rich Stay Wealthy-Total Retirement Freedom, I teach how to create tax wise allocations for distributions when you need income.

If you don't already own this book but would like an extensive explanation you can visit kenhimmler.com/trf and we have a lot of free information on how to design this.

Assuming you're not in need of the income but you're trying to reinvest to grow the money the last thing you want is for taxation to reduce the amount of your reinvestment.

As an example, we'll use a one million-dollar portfolio. Of this portfolio $500,000 of it's in your retirement plan and $500,000 of it's in your non-retirement plan.

Let's further assume you're in a 50-50 allocation. This means you have a 50% stock and a 50% bond blend.

The common way we've seen people structure this type of portfolio is they put $500,000 of stock in the IRA and the $500,000 of bonds in the non-IRA.

The theory goes something like this, the retirement plan is tax-deferred so you should put the higher growth investments in the retirement plan.

This is absolutely _incorrect_ and is an _inefficient_ strategy.

The goal of an IRA or any retirement plan is an arbitrage play. You're trying to invest money today at a high tax rate and take it out later at a lower tax rate.

Remember, you're not trying to get the maximum amount of growth on your retirement plan. If the retirement plan has all the growth, it will cause an increase of your required minimum distributions.

You would prefer the IRA grow at a lower rate and have the non-qualified or non-retirement plan grow at the maximum rate.

I don't want to give you the impression you're intentionally trying to keep the interest or the growth rate on retirement plans low.

I'm stating when you own a balanced portfolio, place the lower returning investments in the retirement plans.

If you're a 100% growth investor, you'll want to segment the high dividend stocks or REIT's from those that are low distribution investments.

Put the high distribution investments into the retirement account to shelter the annual taxation on the dividends or interest.

If you have all growth stocks with no dividends the allocation doesn't matter between the retirement or the non-retirement account.

The low distribution investments would belong in the non-retirement account.

Assuming you believed the stock market will repeat its historical growth of somewhere between 8% to 10% and the bond market will grow somewhere between 4%-6%, you can direct your investments to the right accounts.

Under these assumptions, it makes more sense to put the bonds inside of the retirement plan and the stocks in the non-retirement plan.

If we put the bonds in the non-retirement account, they'll produce interest annually. This interest is paid as taxable income every year whether you spend the interest or not. In addition, the interest is taxable every year to you at ordinary income tax rates.

By you putting the stocks in your non-retirement plan they're not taxed until you sell them.

The other benefit of having the equities in the non-retirement plan is there's no required minimum distributions.

In the non-retirement plan, you can leave the stock or an ETF alone until you decide you want to sell it.

As a note, when I refer to equities, I'm not talking about equity mutual funds.

Equity mutual funds, and all other open-ended mutual funds have a built-in tax problem. They distribute realized gains at the end of the year based upon what the manager buys or sells, which is completely out of your control.

This is one of the many reasons we advise clients to never invest into open-ended mutual funds.

When I refer to stocks and equities I'm talking about individual stocks and equity based ETF's or exchange-traded funds.

What's another downside of putting the equities into a retirement plan?

By putting equities in the retirement plan you should receive maximum growth, which could be counterproductive. This maximum growth will cause two negatives.

The first negative is it will increase your required minimum distributions.

Required minimum distributions are ordinary income taxable and can increase your tax bracket in addition to creating a host of other trigger taxes.

The second negative is when you sell an equity investment inside of a retirement plan You'll eventually pay ordinary income taxes on the investment gain.

If we look at the top ordinary income tax bracket at 39.6% and compare to the top capital gains tax bracket of 20%, the difference is substantial. You'll close to double your tax rate by putting the equities inside your retirement plan.

It's gets worse than just paying a higher bracket on the investment gains. There may be a host of other trigger taxes which catch you.

Most people don't know about these other taxes called trigger taxes. These surprise expenses are because of the growth inside your retirement plan and the amount of the required minimum distributions.

Another reason these taxes are hidden from the retirement plan is they show up on different schedules on your tax returns.

This is a list of the potential trigger taxes a required minimum distribution may cause:

1) Loss of your medical deduction
2) Loss of your mortgage deduction
3) Loss of charitable deductions
4) Alternative Minimum Tax
5) Loss of your property tax deduction
6) Loss of your deductions for investment fees
7) Loss of your deductions for professional fees
8) Increased capital gains tax rates
9) Increased ordinary tax brackets
10) Additional Net Investment Income Tax
11) Additional Medicare premiums
12) Higher taxation on Social Security

How do you fix this tax problem? You must overlay GAMMA, which is a precision way to operate tax allocation. For GAMMA to work it must be consistently reviewed and reallocated.

Would you like to know if your financial advisor and or broker is being lazy? Look at how the investment models are allocated.

If you've invested in an after-tax account (non-retirement) and you also own a retirement account, review what the underlying investments are. If all your accounts are invested in the same underlying positions, then you're definitely NOT using GAMMA.

What the advisor or money manager has done is applied a model or a group of investment picks and bought the same investments in each account.

This is what I call the "assembly line money management strategy."

This is also confirmation your advisor is not practicing GAMMA.

GAMMA is the terminology which explains tax allocation, tax swapping, tax harvesting and even strategic retirement income distribution.

Gamma has gotten a lot of press by mega companies like Morningstar and well known financial writers like Michael Kitces.

Morningstar pegs the additional returns attributable to operating GAMMA at about 1.8% per year or a 29% increase if you're taking income from your portfolio.

If you'd like a detailed explanation of GAMMA, please go to kenhimmler.com/trf to learn more.

If your fiduciary advisor is looking out for your best interests, GAMMA should be used.

Operating GAMMA is an incredible amount of extra work and time. This extra work is how you differentiate a money manager from a fiduciary advisor.

Most money managers or brokers don't normally possess the expertise, the time or have the expensive tools to operate such a system for clients.

The big question is, is your financial advisor or accountant overlaying GAMMA to give you better results?

When you're practicing GAMMA, you're not only following the investments but you're taking advantage of every possible option to reduce tax.

Gamma helps get a higher net take home return with no additional risk.

Let's explain the components of GAMMA:

Tax Allocation

Tax Allocation is placing the right investments into the tax optimized accounts. Even though you may start off with a standard investment allocation model, it doesn't mean the investment positions will keep their original value or allocation percentages. When the allocations or values change you can use the next two GAMMA options.

Tax Swapping

Tax Swapping is when an investment is in one account and there's an opportunity to swap it to another account to get a tax benefit.

You may be familiar with the tax wash rule. This says you cannot sell an investment and buy it back within 30 days and take a tax loss.

We talk about how unfair the tax system is and here yet again is more proof. If you sell an investment for a profit and rebuy it in 29 days, you'll still pay the tax. This is the single edge sword of the IRS.

Prior to 2008, I wrote articles about how to create a tax loss swap with your IRA. In 2008, the IRS issued Revenue Ruling 2008-05 under Section 1091. This new code disallows the swapping between non-retirement and retirement plan accounts. Furthermore, the IRS ruled swapping between any related or controlled party is not allowed.

I wanted to clear up any confusion if you've read earlier books or writings by me. Under tax swapping I'm referring to moving funds in and out of IRA's and or ROTH's and non-retirement accounts.

Let's use an example, assuming Bob has an account with $500,000 in his IRA, $200,000 in his ROTH and $500,000 in his non-retirement account.

The total Bob has across all accounts is $1,200,000.

Inside his IRA he has Johnson and Johnson stock. He bought 1,000 shares at $115 per share. Assuming JNJ has a short-term drop to $85 a share, what can Bob do? Bob can roll out the JNJ to his ROTH and do a ROTH conversion. If it's done correctly he can do this conversion at a tax cost of $85 per share instead of at the tax cost of $115 per share.

Let's use another example. Let's say Bob has required minimum distributions due.

Based on his $500,000, it should be around $20,000 the first year. Instead of taking cash out of the IRA he can take out 235 shares of JNJ.

This will satisfy the required minimum distribution and will allow Bob to keep the stock.

It will allow Bob to reduce his tax cost on the RMD's. The reason is Bob believes JNJ stock is worth $115 per share so this transaction will be tax motivated, not investment motivated.

Based on the difference between the $115 and the $85, Bob's able to save taxes on over $7,000. Bob can move the shares to his non-retirement account and simply hold those shares. If the shares return to the $115.00 per share price he pays no tax unless he sells the shares. If he sells the shares, he would only pay capital gains tax rates on the difference between the $85.00 per share and the $115.00 per share. If he left those same shares in the retirement account, he would have to pay ordinary income tax on the difference between the two share prices or $30.00 per share.

Tax Harvest

When your investment in a stock, bond or mutual fund is at a loss, you're prevented from selling it and repurchasing within thirty days. You can, however, use a replacement option to stay invested in that category.

The IRS defines a wash sale by buying something "substantially identical". They don't provide exact guidance but if you sell SPY (Standard and Poor's S&P 500 ETF) for a loss and immediately repurchase Vanguard Index 500 Mutual Fund, I'm sure they would deny this loss. Even though they're differently issued investments, they're substantially identical.

However, if you sold SPY and bought the S&P 1000, or the Wilshire 500 you'd be able to take the loss as these two securities are not substantially identical.

It's my opinion in the short term, the differences between these replacements are miniscule. After thirty-one days, if you wanted to go back to SPY you could.

One of the other misunderstandings people have is the maximum they can take as an investment tax loss. The common belief is all you can deduct is $3,000 per year.

I've heard many times, "Why go to all this effort if all you can take as a deduction is $3,000?"

The actual rule says your unlimited as to the amount you can deduct each year as long as you have gains to go against the losses.

If you have $50,000 in losses and $50,000 in gains, you can wash out the entire gain against the loss.

If you have $50,000 in losses and only $30,000 in gains, you can use the $30,000 of losses against the gains and still have $20,000 carry over to the next year.

There's no limit on how much in losses you can deduct. There is however a limitation on taking all the losses in one year. You can claim a $3,000 deduction against ordinary income each year on the amount of the capital loss that exceeds the gain until the loss is used up.

This deduction against ordinary income is more valuable than taking the capital loss against a capital gain.

You learned earlier you want to try to stay away from ordinary income tax because the rate is much higher than capital gains tax rates.

What if you take a deduction of ordinary income tax? You're right if you answered you would save more money with an ordinary income tax deduction versus taking a capital loss deduction.

If you take the $3,000 capital loss against ordinary income each year, you're already ahead. With the excess deduction, you can carry it forward to use against future capital gains or simply run it out by using it against ordinary income.

If you remember back in Chapter 5, I discussed using a C Corp. I said there are ways to avoid the double taxation. One of those ways is to build up gains in the Corporation, then use your stock carry forward losses from your personal returns to close down the corporation and bring out all the funds without double taxation.

These *paper* carry forward losses can also be used against future real estate gains.

For years I operated paper loss carry forwards to the point I claimed over $400,000 in personal capital losses.

Years ago I asked one of our new CPA's who worked for me to do my tax returns.

When I asked him to do this he didn't understand why I was asking someone else to do my returns when I was preparing other people's returns.

I explained my time was more valuable doing others people's tax returns rather than my own.

After he reviewed my returns, he came into my office and shut the door. I thought something happened to his dog the way he was beating around the bush.

He finally fessed up and said he'd reviewed my returns and was surprised. He said he found my capital losses and wondered how I was still managing other people's investments if I was such a bad investor?

I explained I actually had unrealized gains on my personal accounts but the paper losses showed differently due to my tax swapping and tax harvesting efforts.

I'm not sure he understood until two years later. I had accumulated about $435,000 in loss carry-forwards from working the harvesting and swapping strategies.

Later, I sold an office building and showed about a $500,000 gain. Can you guess how much gain I paid tax on? If you said out of the $500,000 gain I only paid taxes on about $65,000, you were right.

I was able to use all the loss carry forwards towards the taxable gain.

Another seldom used idea is the corporate tax exclusion strategy.

When you own a C Corporation, you can hold marketable securities within a C corporation. A C Corp is eligible for the corporate dividend tax exclusion. The beauty of the dividend tax exclusion is it allows 70% of your dividends to be tax free.

How many people do you think hold their investments outside of their companies and are paying full taxation on their investments? I would say from my experience, almost everyone holds their investment's outside the C Corp and ends up paying the maximum taxation on the dividends.

Before we conclude this chapter, I want to give you one more tax idea I find being under-utilized. This has to do with life insurance.

As a whole, I believe physicians are one of the biggest believers in life insurance.

The reason I say this is while physicians are the majority of our practice we also deal with successful engineers, dentists, professional athletes, celebrities and business owners.

Out of all these groups I would say physicians are the largest believers in life insurance. It may be because physicians see how fragile and short life is.

The upside of life insurance is if it's used properly it can be a great leveraging tool to pay taxes. It can also protect assets and be utilized as a personal banking system.

The problem with life insurance is if it's cash value life insurance such as whole life or universal life, it takes at least ten years for the cash value to equal the premiums paid in.

If it's variable life, the cash values can lose right along with the stock market so it may never accumulate cash value greater than the premiums paid.

As an example, if you've paid variable life premiums for ten years at a rate of $20,000 per year you've paid in $200,000.

In a non-variable life, you should have a guaranteed $200,000 in cash value. In a variable life you're dependent on the investment markets.

At the end of ten years if the market drops by 50%, your cash value will also drop by 50%. Therefore, if you should have $200,000 in cash value you may only end up with $100,000 in cash value.

While most people don't buy life insurance with the intention of cashing it in, the lower cash value presents a problem.

The estimated cash value must be met. If it's not met you may have to increase your premiums to unaffordable amounts at an older age to avoid the policy lapsing and being left without insurance you've already paid for.

If at the time you decide you don't want to take the risk of a variable life policy and you want to switch to something safer such as whole life, universal life or equity indexed life you can't take a tax deduction on what you lost in the market.

Many variable life owners who have been through a market crash, learned about the extensive fees or have had surprise premium increases are usually the ones wanting to change to something different.

You might also want to change policies if you've bought a whole life, universal life or equity indexed life and you've found a better policy.

The problem is you may not have owned the policy long enough to let the cash value exceed your premiums paid in. In short, you have a loss on your hands.

It's been a long-standing process if you contact your insurance agent and explain you want to switch to a different policy they'll simply do what's called a 1035 exchange.

A 1035 is where one insurance company will do a tax free exchange from your current policy to your new policy.

This 1035 exchange system works when your policy has a taxable gain but not when there's a loss.

You have a potential taxable loss when the basis exceeds the cash value. The basis is the total of all your premiums invested.

To help you understand we'll compare life insurance to real estate.

Let's assume you have a property you've bought for $200,000 and it's now worth $400,000 and you want to exchange for another property, what do you do? You use a 1031 exchange program. This is a tax free exchange from one property to another and it avoids the taxation.

If you've bought the property for $200,000 and it's now worth $150,000, what do you do?

You sell the property for the $150,000 and take a $50,000 tax loss. You then use your sale proceeds to buy a new property.

This all seems so logical when understanding tax exchanges when it's for real estate.

Why is it when someone exchanges one policy for another, the insurance agent uses a 1035 exchange whether the policy is at a gain or a loss?

Might it be because the insurance agent doesn't realize you can in fact deduct a loss on a life insurance policy?

There's a mid-step which must be taken in order for you to take advantage of this.

Let's use an example. For this we'll assume you've invested $200,000 in your life insurance policy.

We'll also assume this is a variable life and between the market drops and the excessive fees you now only have $100,000 in cash value.

Let's further assume the insurance agent has shown you the new design of an equity indexed life policy.

This new policy has the same death benefit as your current policy. It also has the same premiums but has no risk and has a guarantee that they can never raise your premiums.

Last, it has a long-term care rider which would pay the death benefit while you're alive if needed for medical care.

With your decision of wanting to switch policies, what do you do next?

The insurance agent tells you to 1035 the $100,000 from your old policy to the new policy.

What just happened? You lost a $100,000 ordinary income tax deduction.

How then do you get this deduction? You 1035 the old variable life policy into a short-term one-year annuity. After one year and one day you cash out the annuity. You can now take an ordinary income tax deduction of $100,000.

This isn't a capital gains tax deduction where you're limited to $3,000 a year. This is an ordinary deduction which can be used against all your other income. The deduction is technically referred to as a 4797 loss.

How does this work?

Life insurance is never allowed a tax deduction for losses but annuities are.

You're allowed to 1035 exchange from an annuity to life insurance, not the other way around. To be clear, you may not 1035 from an annuity to a life insurance policy.

If you 1035 from the life insurance to the annuity and hold for at least one year and one day you can cash out of the annuity.

The annuity will hold the same basis as your life insurance. If your life insurance had a $200,000 cost basis, so will the annuity.

If the life insurance has a $100,000 cash value so will the annuity.

When you cash out of the annuity, your basis will be $200,000 and the cash value will be $100,000.

This is how you get the $100,000 loss.

CHAPTER 9. WHERE TO GO FROM HERE?

By now you have a better idea of some of the obstacles and challenges you'll face in your fight to hold onto more of what you make.

I'll share one parting note. Financial plans, tax plans, and any type of "plan" is a nebulous term to most. To help you understand what it means to have a "plan" I'll relate it to an experience you might have had.

If you're old enough, you may remember when AAA used to give you a Trip-Tic. This was that nifty little plastic bound map that was in the size of a brochure.

All you had to do is to go to the AAA office and tell them where you wanted to go. The agent would pull these little brochure size maps out of a large organizer and assemble your trip for you.

This was of course long before GPS's or smart phones with Google Maps.

When the agent would assemble these maps, they'd take a highlighter and draw the most efficient route to get to your destination.

129

If there happened to be road construction or speed traps they'd take their red pen and mark a big X so you'd be prepared. If it was major construction they'd reroute your trip to save you some time.

That's how I'd always travel because I'm a planner. I like to map out the route and see if there's a more time or cost efficient way of getting to the destination.

What I've found is some people will just jump in their car for a road trip without a plan.

They'll have a general idea of where they want to go but no plan.

Along the way they'll roll down their window and ask some stranger on the street where to go or how to get there.

In most cases the stranger on the street doesn't know any better where they are or how they can help someone else get to where they want to go.

It's not much different than how people map out their tax plan, their retirement plan, their investment plan or sometimes anything in their lives.

When it comes to people's investments, retirement and tax plans most people just trod along thinking it will just magically happen and it'll all work out for the best.

During their working years and even into retirement they'll ask the banker, the accountant or the insurance guy how to get where they want to go.

This is the same as jumping in your car with no plan and just asking people along the way directions on how to get to your destination.

You can see why so many smart people don't get to their destinations.

I'm a huge believer in mapping out plans, testing, and then testing again before you make any decision.

This relates back to the three golden rules of financial success.

CALCULATE
CALCULATE
CALCULATE

Now that I've given you the Trip-Tic example you're ready to see what options you have.

I wanted to use that example because the people that remember Trip-Tics are fading.

Onto what your options are on how to improve your financial situation.

1) Do it yourself.
If you'd like to go down the road of doing it yourself, then you'll need tools and processes to do your calculations.

In my most recent book, **Live Rich Stay Wealthy - Total Retirement Freedom**, I unveil the processes most successful financial planners use. I also give the tools to use and how to use them.

If you're an avid do - it - yourself person, this is a must read.

You can go to <u>kenhimmler.com/buylrswtrf</u> to order the book or go to Amazon and search for Live Rich Stay Wealthy.

There's a few books I've written so if you're looking for the do-it-yourself version, buy the **<u>Total Retirement Freedom</u>** book.

For a list of resources, you can also go to <u>kenhimmler.com/trf</u> and there are available resources to find out just about anything you need to know to put your plan together.

2) Hire it out.

If you're like me, you like to hire experts to figure out things you're not an expert at.

If this sounds like you, you can go to kenhimmler.com/coach and you can schedule a complimentary call with one of our expert coaches.

During this phone conference they'll give you a second opinion on your tax, investment, trust, entity, business structure and risk protection plan. Depending on your situation they may also grant you access to our online analysis program.

I hope this book has educated and informed you to the point where you'll take action.

As I always do, I like to provide a little motivation to get you to take action.

Imagine a new patient came to you. When you walk into the room, you see he's about one hundred pounds' overweight. He's holding a vodka in one hand and a cigarette in the other. He tells you he's interested in improving his health.

What are the first actions you would tell him to take? Hopefully, it would be to stop drinking and stop smoking.

You, as a concerned and caring doctor would also give him a little motivation by telling him the risks of not stopping these bad habits.

The best doctors I've met are the ones which give real-life examples of telling the patient how and what they would put their family through and what could be expected of continuing these bad habits.

While my calling is nowhere near as important as what a physician does, the improvement of someone's financial security can improve their life and their family's lives.

So here it goes: If you're working forty hours a week and you're earning $200,000 a year, you're earning $100 per hour.

What if you're missing out on tax benefits of just 10% of your income? This small percentage would amount to $20,000 a year? This loss can be looked at in two ways, time loss or future value of money loss.

If we view your missed opportunities in the aspect of time, you must work 200 hours every year, just to make up for the money you're losing out on.

Where would you rather spend this time?

Who would you rather spend this time with?

If we view your missed opportunities as money, then a $20,000 investment could do the following:

- Buy a vacation home worth $150,000

- Have an account worth $279,000 in ten years at only a 6% rate of return

- Lease two Mercedes-Benz automobiles

- Fully educate two children for college

- Pay for a nanny

- Pay for a full-time house cleaner

- Finally, for $20,000 a year, you could take one heck of a nice vacation every year.

In summary, the money is better off **in your pocket** than the IRS's pocket or some financial institutions coffers.

In closing, thank you for your sacrifice and dedication in becoming a physician. I only wish there were more of you!

Made in the USA
Columbia, SC
22 April 2022

59330492R00083